Cryptocurrency

The Easy Guide to Bitcoin Investing & Blockchain Cryptocurrency Understanding

(Profitability in the Digital Currency Revolution Revealed)

Samual Deleon

TABLE OF CONTENT

Bitcoin Exchanges And Markets 1

What To Watch Out For In A Transaction 2

What Is Cryptocurrency? 8

Shitcoins With Potential As Good Investments 32

Why Bitcoin May Be A Good Investment 54

How Do Cryptocurrencies Work? 66

Blockchain, Mining, And Ico: A New Technological Paradigm 89

Chapter 1: Money Talks 122

How Do Digital Currencies Function? 139

What Products Can You Buy Using Cryptocurrencies? 149

How To Understand Cryptocurrencies 152

Consider Investing. Think Of Bitcoin This Way 172

Reasons Bitcoin Prices Are So Variable 185

Bitcoin Exchanges And Markets

You must utilize a cryptocurrency exchange if you want to buy or sell cryptocurrency. These online services typically perform the role of stockbrokers by giving you access to tools for purchasing and promoting virtual currencies like bitcoins, ethereum, and other cryptocurrencies. With affordable exchange rates and strong security features, the best cryptocurrency exchanges make it simple to purchase and sell your preferred currencies.

Consider the collaborating currencies, pricing, withdrawal options, and security we focused on in our list of the best cryptocurrency exchanges when choosing the best exchange for your needs. Check out the exchangers directly to learn which ones are probably the best for your needs.

What To Watch Out For In A Transaction

Access

Due to regional or national regulations, you may not be able to purchase or advertise cryptocurrencies on specific exchanges depending on where you are. A few nations, including China, have outlawed their citizens' access to cryptocurrency exchanges.

There is a great deal of regulatory ambiguity about cryptocurrencies in the US, and just a few states have established their own legislation. For instance, in order to sell recognized coins, businesses in New York need licenses. While most states no longer have laws as harsh as those in New York, several have changed their laws or are taking measures to do so. The national conference of legislators reports that 31 states have proposed legislation governing virtual currencies for the 2021 legislative sessions.

Security

Since there is no centralized authority behind cryptocurrencies, they are less secure than traditional investments or bank accounts. Any USD balance for some exchanges, like Coinbase and Gemini, is kept in FDIC-insured bank accounts. However, the FDIC does not cover cryptocurrency balances.

A few exchanges have insurance policies in place to safeguard your cryptocurrency against fraud or hacking that can affect the digital currencies that users keep on the exchange. For instance, Coinbase has a $255 million insurance policy. As a result, the owners of the accounts may be protected if Coinbase's reserves were compromised and any amount up to $255 million was stolen. Others, like Kraken, rely more on security measures than insurance coverage to safeguard clients.

The security of the exchange should be a high priority, regardless of whether you want to retain your cryptocurrency holdings there permanently or only keep them there temporarily before transferring them to your wallet. Check, for instance, how long the exchange retains its assets in hard storage.

The value of cryptocurrency will rise as higher prices approach more lucrative targets for capacity thieves, making this even more crucial.

There were 28 attacks on the cryptocurrency industry in 2020, with

KuCoin, a Singapore-based exchange, suffering the highest loss of $200 million.

Count the number of properties the trade owns offline. Even though exchanges by their very nature require some crypto to be enabled in order to facilitate trade, it's wise to keep the majority of holdings offline or in a bloodless garage, where access by hackers is more difficult. For instance, Coinbase claims that it maintains 98% of user assets offline, with the smallest 2% engaging in active trading. This addition gives you even more reason to rely on your cryptocurrency in the event of a hack, in addition to its $255 million coverage.

Additionally, you may see conventional online security measures like two-factor authentication that you may already be accustomed to on other platforms. This implies that in addition to your username and password, you will also need to enter another method of identity verification, such as entering the code you receive through text message each time you log in.

These days, you can feel secure operating in well-known exchanges with a sizable consumer base. Doing business with small or new exchanges that lack online offers and security measures puts you at danger.

"Size Matters Here," asserts Douglas Bonparth, financial advisor and head of Bon Fide Wealth in New York. He makes reference to Coinbase, which is currently quite popular at the Nasdaq stock exchange. It has advantages and cons, but now that you have access to public finances, you can assess the agency's financial stability, which is crucial when engaging in business or investing in a provider of goods or services. Consider the assistance they are offering.

Fees Although they are something to think about, a larger cost structure need not prevent you from trading. The founder of Uinta Crypto Consulting, a course for novice investors to learn about cryptocurrencies, Spencer Montgomery, claims: "The easier they make it for you to buy, the higher the fees you will pay." Higher fees can also be a worthwhile trade-off for the extra security and insurance that larger, more well-liked exchanges offer.

Exchange rates could be a fixed fee, but they're typically a percentage of your change. Some exchanges, like the coins app, base their fee pricing primarily on price swings. Depending on whether you are a buyer or a seller, costs are frequently assessed according to the transaction. Depending on the currencies you switch between, there can be additional fees. Before transferring your coins in your cryptocurrency transactions, be sure you understand how and when the trade wants to price you.

What Is Cryptocurrency?

There are two types of endpoints connected by a P2P protocol in the world of cryptography. The first is a typical public node, and the second is a miner's node. Consider it to be a web, with each node acting as a junction. Every node has a few direct connections to other nodes, but eventually all nodes are linked together indirectly.

Nodes

A node is a single occurrence of an address on a single computer. It is feasible to set up a single computer to act as numerous nodes, but a causal user is unlikely to do this. One node is simply taken to be one machine at the end of a P2P network in this book. A network must have at least two nodes to be considered one. Approximately 12000 nodes on the Bitcoin network are active at any given time as of this writing. More may exist, but many of them may be kept inactive and hence undetectable by the scan that was launched to find them.

Two categories of public nodes exist. One node is for common users, and the other is for light users. The former has complete blockchain data. The latter only provides the condensed form of the ledger that is pertinent to the coins kept in that account.

The full ledger node and the light node, which simply has the ledger of the currencies that relate to it, are the two different types of regular nodes.

Although the P2P protocol can be used without the internet, it performs best when connected. A P2P network is just a collection of computers connected to one another directly over a single open port. This relationship travels straight between the user nodes and doesn't require a server. Only specified data that is contained in the ledger can be sent to you via that port on the node by the other party.

So don't be concerned if someone breaks in and steals your information or if you are hacked. That still requires some effort, and it won't happen unless the penetrator has a strong sense of motivation.

Your software makes a comparison between the ledger that is stored on your machine and the shared ledger. In the event of a discrepancy, it then awaits the ledger of a few other nodes.

The way that various cryptos handle the general behavior varies slightly. However, in general, you can choose how many nodes to connect to in order to receive ledger changes.

Block A

Blocks represent the information that is stored in the nodes. A block contains a number of transactions. The range of that number is between 1000 and 2500. There is a website that keeps tabs on a block's typical transactions. There is no restriction on the number of transactions that can be included in a block, but there is one on the size of the block, and it can even be as low as one. Each block in the Bitcoin protocol can only be 1 to 2 MB in size. This is hard-coded. Other cryptos will have different restrictions.

A transaction forms a chain with the block that came before it and will continue to do so for the blocks that are added after it once a block has been added, hashed, and entered into record.

Typically, one block contains the details of all the transactions that are contained within it. It includes the hash of the previous block as well as a few other pieces of data, such as the node that produced the hash, etc. However, the fact that the block contains the hash of the preceding block is what matters most.

Each transaction in the block is entered into a computer procedure, where they are iterated again and over again until they yield a predetermined string of letters. This is a non-random, one-way cryptographic hash that only functions in one direction. As a result, the same string will always be produced when the same data is entered into the block and hashed. But even a small alteration will have a big impact on the entire hash string. This will be revealed later on in the novel.

If A paid B, C paid D, and F paid G, all of those transactions would be gathered into one block and added to the record of transactions already in existence.

The block is then hashed (we'll learn how that works in the following chapter), and this hash is then added to the publicly accessible record.

When a block is hashed and accepted by the network, a chain is formed because, as you may recall, each block has the hash of the block before it, and the block after that will include the hash of the block before it. As a result, one block is added to the block that came before it, and this information can be traced back to the Genesis Block, the very first block ever made.

Innuendo Protocol

The P2P network operates on an automatic gossip protocol and communicates frequently with its neighbors to learn whether they are aware of what it is aware of. It will broadcast the new information if the neighbor has less information than it does. The neighbor will provide updates if they have any fresh information. Each node links at random to six other nodes on average, making it a rather efficient system. It only takes seven (really fewer) steps to propagate the most recent blockchain across the complete network of 12,000 nodes if each node links to six other nodes and transmits its information to them, and each of those six nodes are then linked to six more and pass that information along.

The most recent information can quickly propagate across all available nodes thanks to data propagation in a gossip network using a P2P foundation. It takes between ten and thirty minutes to confirm any transaction. Therefore, even if A were to transmit money to B halfway over the world, the transaction could be finished in a matter of seconds and verified in under an hour.

Depending on the volume of traffic and the speed of your internet connection, it can take a new node up to 24 hours to download the complete ledger onto the computer. Updates happen quickly once you have the most recent version of the ledger, and you are always free to turn off your computer. Then, when you restart it, it will look for and find any updates that have been made since the last time.

All crypto nodes have automated processes.

Ledger

There was a ledger that the bank kept, as you could see in the bank or fiat currency example with Mr. A, Ms. B, and Mrs. C. Who maintains the ledger now that you are aware that there is no central authority in cryptocurrencies? Well, most of you are aware of that component. Each person has a copy of the ledger, which is set up as a chain of transactions connected by links. When a transaction is made, for example, Mr. A might give Ms. B a crypto coin for the same amount as a cheque for $20. The transaction is then added to a shared ledger that is accessible to the entire network.

In contrast to the bank example, this ledger is now decentralized rather than centralized. The obvious advantage of such is that if one party loses the ledger, there will automatically be several copies available to recreate the data.

Your cryptocurrency app checks the status of the coins you own and displays the balance on your screen after logging in to the network. The number (the balance) that is displayed to you is actually taken from the complete, active blockchain, not just from what your node recalls it to be.

Every node will bear witness to your possession of the coins you hold if you do this. What occurs then when you use your coin? You can use both the public key and the private key at this point. Before we do that, though, allow me to briefly describe a hash so you can understand what a private key and public key are as well as the fundamentals of mining.

When you fully comprehend a hash, you can see the reasoning behind what happens when you begin mining. However, don't worry if you don't comprehend anything using hashes or keys. You can continue to mine cryptocurrencies.

Hash

Be prepared to be perplexed. Hash can be defined in a few different ways. In everyday speech, the term "hash" simply refers to the character string created by combining all of the input data.

But in reality, the term "hash" refers to the process of reducing data of any size to a fixed number of characters after being crunched. This hash is often performed using asymmetric cryptography, which is a one-way street.

This means that after entering the original document, you will receive a hash or digest. However, you won't be able to find the content of the source document if you try to reverse that digest.

Passwords are saved on websites in this manner. A password must be entered when setting up an account, like your online bank account. After that, the password is hashed and kept on the bank's encrypted files. When you log in to your account and enter your password, that password is again hashed and compared to the hash that is already stored. You get access if they match. If not, well, you already know the rest. The key is that the passwords stored on the discs are hashes rather than precise passwords, so if malicious individuals gain access to the bank's computers and steal their password file, they won't be able to reverse-engineer it.

The elegance of hashes is that. You cannot use an algorithm to recover the original text from a hash.

Point to Recall: Bear in mind that a hash generator will return a string of characters that looks like this after processing any size of file:

The full text of the national anthem has been hashed using the MD5 algorithm. If you want to test it out for yourself, go ahead and give it a shot. You can use Google to find a "online MD5 hash generator" and then type whatever you want into it after you find one. The hash generator will chew on it and output a defined length whether it is a single word or a passage long enough to fill a book.

The resulting hash will vary if you make even the smallest modification. The period at the very end of the lyrics in the aforementioned example was simply omitted, and the result is the hash seen below:

Nothing but the most recent period was removed between the two, although the current hash created differs greatly from the original. However, if you repeatedly hash the same information, you will obtain the same hash.

Secure Hash Algorithm 256 bit, or SHA256, is the algorithm used by Bitcoin. Because it would require more processing power to break than is now accessible on the planet, the chances of penetrating it are remote. Therefore, it would be impossible to crack the SHA256 until someone develops a method of computing that uses no energy.

You will learn more about the hash's properties as the book progresses and you gain a practical understanding of hashes and mining.

Recap

Before moving on, let's just put everything in perspective so that we can comprehend what cryptocurrencies are and what fundamental components and processes are at work.

Cryptographic tokens with predetermined values that can be transmitted across nodes in a transaction are known as cryptocurrencies. These tokens can be sent electronically and don't require any physical components to represent them. These strings of text, which can be viewed objectively, are your coins. The first component is that.

The second component is the blockchain, which is made up of the transactional underpinnings that grant each coin its legitimacy. The record of the ledger covering the lifespan of the coin and the entire cryptocurrency is contained in the block chain. One cryptocurrency, Bitcoin, has a blockchain on which all bitcoin transactions are recorded.

The nodes make up the third component. Without the node network, the blockchain cannot be considered a valid record, making it impossible to establish whether a coin is real or not. Because there are copies of the record on various independent nodes, it is legitimate.

The miner is the very last and final component of bitcoin. Despite the fact that the mining is the book's focus, we haven't yet discussed it. The node that creates the hashes recorded in the blockchain is known as a miner. The hashes cannot be computed without the miner, which causes the blockchain to stop working.

Every node normally contains a wallet, and each node is free to have as many wallets or as many accounts in a single wallet as it desires. In cryptography, they are sometimes referred to as addresses rather than accounts. That is very similar to an email address, however it is a string of characters instead.

Wallets

It's not the leather binding you keep stashed in your handbag or back pocket. An app called a wallet can assist you in performing several tasks. It produces an address for you initially based on the specifications of the crypto you're using. You offer your counterpart who is paying you this address.

Private Keys

The wallet creates a random number before trying to obtain an address. The beginning is here. This random number complies with the rules established by the wallet for the cryptocurrency it supports. Take Bitcoin, for instance. Its value can range from 1 to Its representation in hexadecimal notation is as follows: between 0x1 and 0xFFFFFFFF FFFFFFFF FFFFFFFE BAAEDCE6 AF48A03B BFD25E8C D0364140.

The most crucial component of this is the private key, which needs to be handled with the same care as your safe's keys.

Private Keys

The next step in the process of generating an address is the public key. Since this public key is obtained from the private key, a random integer within the previously specified range is really selected and processed. This method, which involves elliptic curves and is outside the purview of this book, is a mathematical operation. But the outcome of that operation is a string of characters.

Personal Keys

This relationship is asymmetrical. 2E96 public keys can exist for a single private key, but only one private key can exist for one public key. Therefore, the only method to decode it is to test each key against the public key that is visible. You would have to try 2E96 different combinations, or 7.92 x 10E28, in order to be able to read the private key if you did this. The public/private key pair is safe for this reason.

Currency Address

Once the private key has been created, it is taken and hashed once more using the public key to produce a string of integers. This is the Bitcoin address you provide to others so they can send you money.

Invoice Balance

Someone could give you money after they know your address and your private key, but it wouldn't show up in your wallet. However, because the sender informed your wallet, your wallet is unaware that it was sent to you. Not at all. Your wallet constantly reads the ledger that contains all the transactions in almost real-time, so it is able to tell when money has reached you. It displays the balance in the account when it detects a transaction containing your address.

Once a coin has been delivered to a specific address, it can only be spent by someone who also has access to the account's private key. If they don't, the blockchain community won't accept the money's redirection, keeping the coin's block chain, or ownership record, unchanged. Every transaction that appears in the ledger is actually just a record of who owns which coin at the time.

Blockchain

Now that you are familiar with the transaction, let's talk about the blockchain.

Let me go back to a previous step first. We saw that the nodes communicate with one another when we initially looked at them. Every time you complete a transaction, a broadcast of that transaction is transmitted to every other node. When those nodes take it up, they transmit it to additional nodes, one of which will eventually be a miner's node.

This transaction is taken by a miner, who adds it to a block. Other miners that receive this pending transaction also include it in a block at the same time. A given transaction is being processed by several miners simultaneously as part of various blocks. They begin to tackle a resource-intensive puzzle after they group several transactions together. This means that they combine a number of different components, including the transactions they have picked, with the hash of the most recent block in the chain. Then they attempt to solve a puzzle that is meant to produce a hash inside a specific range. The difficulty of this is actually much greater than it appears, and we shall discuss this in more detail as the book progresses.

The first miner to attain 51% of the current nodes will validate their block, fall off, and attempt the next block after the block puzzle has been solved. Any transactions that don't fit into this block will be left as pending transactions. The next miner to attempt a block pulls it and attempts to solve the following conundrum.

The system will immediately send the miner's Bitcoin address with the bitcoins as payment after he has solved the challenge and the network has approved it.

These bitcoins are entirely fresh and have never been used. These are created by the system as a compensation for the miners' efforts in processing the blocks that are added to the blockchain.

Shitcoins With Potential As Good Investments

Numerous initiatives relating to cryptocurrencies give the market little to no value. Memecoins, or "shitcoins," as some like to call them, are currently fashionable. Shitcoins are generally thought of as not having a clear value or function and as falling under no one category. These coins can have a very low or no market value. The majority of shitcoins get value by just existing or by asking a well-known person or group to support them. These currencies have a strong network of long-term supporters, a quality product to offer, and a successful marketing strategy. This book contains a list of the top shitcoins that could make you rich in 2023 and beyond.

SafeMoon

SafeMoon Protocol is a decentralized finance (DeFi) coin. According to the company's website, SafeMoon performs three processes throughout each deal: Reflection, LP Acquisition, and Burn. The Safemoon coin was released in March 2021 and quickly gained popularity. It claims to be the coin with the fastest growth rate even if it is useless in real life. If you want to invest in cryptocurrencies for less than $1 US, Safemoon can be a great choice.

Dogelon Mars (Elon) comedy coin with a dog theme Available on both Ethereum and Polygon is Dogelon Mars. It is based on several well-known canine coins, including Dogecoin, Shiba Inu, and Floki Inu.

Dogelon Mars uses a variety of popular meme coin themes. Dogecoin and Elon Musk, a well-known supporter of Doge and a multibillionaire businessman, were combined to create its name.

Infant Doge Coin

Baby Doge is lovely but has a lot of BITE! Baby Doge is a deflationary token that will gradually become more and more rare. All Baby Doge holders will instantly receive more Baby Doge only by retaining your coins in your wallet. You may observe the amount of baby dogecoin in your wallet grow as holders automatically earn a 5% fee from each on-chain transaction that occurs on the Baby Doge ecosystem. The amount of baby doge coins that the community receives is increased by the fees that are paid during each transaction.

Toki Floki

Floki Inu (FLOKI), a meme coin with a dog theme, refers to itself as "a movement" rather than a meme coin. It is a cryptocurrency that was developed by supporters and members of the Shiba Inu (SHIB) community. The coin pays tribute to Elon Musk's Shiba Inu.

Despite his apparent assertions that he possesses any SHIB, Musk is a well-known advocate of Dogecoin.

Dogecoin

Dogecoin (DOGE), which is based on the well-known "Doge" Internet joke, has a Shiba Inu as its logo. The open-source digital currency was produced through the forking of Litecoin in December 2013 by Billy Markus from Portland, Oregon, and Jackson Palmer from Sydney, Australia. Dogecoin is one of the best shitcoins to purchase in 2022.

1" Network

The 1inch Network offers a number of decentralized protocols, whose cooperation makes it possible for DeFi operations to be as efficient, rapid, and safe as possible.

The 1inch Network's original protocol is a decentralized exchange (DEX) aggregator solution that finds deals across a variety of liquidity sources and provides customers with better prices than any single exchange.

Samoyed Currency SAMO is a brand-new internet resource that promotes a community devoted to uniting Solana users, enlightening industry participants, establishing connections, and helping one another overcome obstacles in life. We are the quickest, most potent, and eco-friendly dog coin in the game, but we want to be MORE than that—we want to be Solana's representative.

(LUNC) Terra Classic

This coin wasn't intended to be a shitcoin from the beginning. Since the item's community has disintegrated, it isn't really useful for anything else.

LUNC is the primary resource of the original Terra blockchain and stablecoin ecosystem. The asset, which formerly traded on the stock exchange under the symbol "LUNA," was one of the biggest cryptocurrencies that could be purchased. Everything changed after the Terra biosphere's failure in May.

Right now, LUNC is not very beneficial. It remains one of the best shitcoins currently in circulation. The price of LUNC, which is currently $0.0001071, has climbed by 3.78% from yesterday.

The entire ecosystem, including LUNC, collapsed after Terra's UST stablecoin was depegged. Eventually, Terra's creators implemented a hard fork, moving the entire ecosystem to a new blockchain that was backed by a new asset.

Despite being largely dormant, LUNC still evokes powerful feelings among many investors. Many investors have shown interest in the asset because they believe there is still a chance for a rise and a return for them. Investors looking for low-risk returns with a chance of long-term gains may consider this coin.

Dogs of Elon (DOE) Dogs Of Elon is an additional choice for people looking for the best shitcoins currently on the market. The asset has totally taken over the shtick market despite only making its debut in December 2021. In an effort to become one of the most well-known shitcoins, Dogs Of Elon, which is also named after the Tesla CEO, is using an innovative marketing tactic.

DOE is related to the NFT television show "Dogs of Elon." The collection has distinct sub-collections with 30 unique Elon NFTs and 70 zombie Doges, as well as 10,000 dog-themed NFTs.

Given the success of the NFTs industry, it is easy to see why DOE is gaining ground. The asset is currently trading at $0.0176, down 3.46% over the previous 24 hours but up a healthy 5% over the previous week.

TOKEN KISHU INU PITBULL PIG

APE NFT HOGE POLYDOGE FEG TOKEN

LUFFIN AS SQUACK

The following are the results: SAITAMA CATGIRL YOOSHI VINU VOLT INU SOS BRISE SAFEMARS UFO WIN

Exchange tokens are also something I advise due of their applications. It is advised to purchase them at the extremely low cost. The trading activity on those exchanges increases as the price of bitcoin rises, increasing the value of the exchange tokens. BNB, Gate.io, Whitebit, MEXC, Hotbit, Trust wallet, Bakery, and more premium exchange tokens are available for purchase.

These tokens have the potential to increase in value soon.

Cryptocurrency is defined as a digital currency where encryption code is utilized to decide and control how currency units are created as well as to confirm electronic payment transfers. It operates independent of any bank's purview.

A sort of tradeable cash that could be utilized online between two people without the involvement of a third party, like a bank, was the premise behind cryptocurrencies.

The term "Cryptocurrency" was initially used by a user of the "Bitcoin Forum," liked by the project's creators, and then adopted by the general public.

The Development of Cryptocurrencies

Before Bitcoin, there was 1998–2009

There were attempts to develop various concepts for digital currencies that were encrypted before Bitcoin, which was the first cryptocurrency to be fully created.

The growth of online trade was starting to accelerate. It was essential to use a third party financial institution, such as a bank, credit card company, or service like PayPal, in order to make electronic payments. This is OK for the majority of transactions, but it may come with additional expenses and dangers. A transaction may be halted or reversed. Physical money, often known as Fiat money, can be used to purchase goods and services in the non-digital world. Therefore, there is no middleman involved. The digital world, however, made this impossible.

It was necessary to develop an electronic payment system that allowed two parties to transact with one another directly and was based on cryptographic proof rather than trust. It was essential to make sure that these transactions, once completed, couldn't be undone in order to safeguard both the buyer and the seller against fraud.

B-money was the initial suggestion. It was developed by Wei Dai, an American computer engineer who worked on cryptography research at the Microsoft Corporation in Redmond, Washington. Soon after, a different method called Bit Gold was proposed by computer scientist and cryptographer Nick Szabo. Despite the fact that neither proposal received official approval, the core concepts were used to develop the first cryptocurrency, bitcoin.

2008 to 2009: Bitcoin's Evolution

On August 18, 2008, the domain name bitcoin.org was originally registered.

A document titled "Bitcoin: A Peer to Peer Electronic Cash System," was uploaded to a discussion email list on the topic of cryptography on October 31, 2008. Although the writers of this document claimed to be Satoshi Nakamoto, their real identities are still a mystery.

The Bitcoin network was created when Satoshi first made the software accessible to the entire public in January 2009. In an effort to spark interest in the concept, the software offered free bitcoins to anyone who downloaded it. The first bitcoin block was mined by Satoshi. The "The Genesis Block" carried a reward of 50 bitcoins and was referred to as such.

Since nobody was interested in the concept at the time, the project initially stalled. However, this was about to change when Martti Malmi, commonly known as Sirius, a solitary student at Finland's Helsinki University of Technology, came upon the Bitcoin.org website and developed an interest in the concept behind it. Martti emailed Satoshi in May 2009 and offered to help develop Bitcoin further. Within a few weeks of this initial communication, Martti's suggestions had completely overhauled the Bitcoin website. The C++ code that Satoshi had used to create Bitcoin was then taught to him by himself. Martti soon rose to prominence as Bitcoin's primary developer and started the Bitcoin forum. The phrase "cryptocurrency" was used in a forum post by a user, and Satoshi, Martti, and other users loved it so much that they continued to use it.

A proponent of bitcoin was Hal Finney, a video game creator who earned an engineering degree from Caltech in 1981. On the first day of the program's release, he downloaded it and was paid 10 bitcoins. This was the first-ever bitcoin transaction in history.

Before ending his participation, Satoshi is thought to have mined about 1 million bitcoins.

2010: Bitcoin's value increases

Bitcoins had only been mined up to this time; they had not yet been traded. This implied that there was no way to assign them any kind of monetary exchange value. That is, until someone made the decision to buy two pizzas with his bitcoins. In the exchange, he traded 10,000 bitcoins, making those two pizzas the most costly takeout order ever, according to today's value.

On August 6, 2010, it was revealed that some transactions had not been properly vetted before being added to the transaction log (blockchain), which was a significant issue with Bitcoin. This meant that users could essentially get around the limitations on the number of bitcoins that could be generated. Due to this, two addresses displayed on the network generated almost 184 billion. The issue was soon resolved after the transaction was found and deleted from the logs. It is the sole issue that has ever arisen in the history of bitcoin.

The introduction of new cryptocurrencies between 2011 and 2012

As Bitcoin became more and more well-known, new cryptocurrencies started to emerge. Examples include Litecoin and Namecoin. These new cryptocurrencies frequently promised higher encryption, faster speeds, and other benefits in an effort to outperform Bitcoin. There are currently more than a thousand of these coins, often known as altcoins (alternatives to Bitcoin), and the number is only expected to grow over time.

New iterations of Bitcoin's software, now known as Bitcoin Core, kept coming out during this time.

2013 saw the price collapse of bitcoin.

Over $1,000 is paid for each coin of bitcoin. A few days later, China states that its financial institutions, including banks, are not permitted to accept bitcoins. They did this because they disapproved of unofficial cash and believed it should not be used in commerce. Market panic ensued as a result of people's concern that other nations might follow suit. A Bitcoin's price crashed, and it took more than two years for it to climb back to its pre-crash level.

With the inclusion of numerous more pages and other functionality, the

Bitcoin website was upgraded to take on its current format. The translation system was developed in order to increase global accessibility of the website.

Illegal activities in 2014

Many people utilize a bitcoin exchange to enable the quick exchange of bitcoins. This is an online market that connects buyers and sellers. Most people agree that these exchanges are the safest venues to convert bitcoins for other fiat currencies ($, £, €). It is an entirely online marketplace that serves as a middleman between potential buyers and sellers. BTC or XBT is the accepted acronym for the bitcoin currency.

One of the biggest bitcoin exchanges in the world at the time, MT Gox, vanished over night in January 2014. The owners of the 850,000 bitcoins that were traded at the time lost them forever. The inquiry into this is still underway, but it's still unclear exactly what transpired on that day. Whatever the truth of that tale, $450 million worth of bitcoins were stolen. They would be worth more like $4.5 billion now.

The introduction of Ethereum and ICOs in 2016.

Ethereum is the only other cryptocurrency that has, as of yet, come close to matching the success of Bitcoin. That utilizes a system called Ether. Initial Coin Offerings, or ICOs, started to surface on fundraising sites almost at the same time. In the same way that they let investors to invest in and trade cryptocurrencies, they give them the chance to trade start-up businesses, frequently in the form of stocks and shares. Given that ICOs might be frauds created by criminals to seem as legal investments, this is considered to be a risky investment. As a result, the Chinese government outright prohibited them.

2017 and Beyond: Cryptocurrency's Continued Growth and Popularity

Spending your Bitcoins has been simpler over time as more merchants start to accept them as a form of payment. It is predicted that additional cryptocurrencies will also be accepted as a form of legal money, and that you will soon be able to use them to make purchases in neighborhood shops.

Numerous banking institutions, especially those with headquarters in Europe, are currently considering how they may get engaged in the trading of cryptocurrencies. They see the size of the market and, understandably, want a piece of the action.

Whatever you think of cryptocurrencies, it would seem that they are definitely here to stay. They have been called anything from the future of money to a complete fraud. Some even believe they will displace conventional currency.

Although there are numerous applications for cryptocurrencies, only Bitcoin and Ethereum have received widespread acceptance to date. Here are some examples to help you get an idea of what you can do with your coins:

Travel the world and buy all the extras, like flights, hotels, car rentals, or even cruises; Buy precious metals like gold or platinum; Buy or sell luxury items, from artwork to jewelry; Pay for your kids' university educations; Use a Bitcoin ATM to withdraw money from your Bitcoin virtual money wallet; Use Bitpay at an increasing number of merchant locations.

You might be perplexed as to how Bitcoin can be used to pay for a coffee when one Bitcoin is worth so much more. The appeal of cryptocurrencies is that, unlike traditional money, you are not limited to using them in accordance with their single unit value. Because it is digital money, just a small portion of the value of a single coin can be spent.

Why Bitcoin May Be A Good Investment

In the context of digital money and cryptocurrency, what exactly is investing?

Cryptocurrency is an asset that may be purchased or acquired with the potential for value growth over time, much like any other sort of investment, including foreign cash, precious metals, stocks, and shares.

The benefits of cryptocurrencies as a long-term investment are possible. This is possible as long as you are willing to keep your investment for a long time. Trading will be a superior technique to make money if you want to have the chance to make a return on your investment quickly. Trading is a method of generating consistent, though modest, returns. For more details, please refer to chapter 10.

Cryptocurrency might theoretically be compared to any other form of money (fiat money), which we are all familiar with. This implies that it can be used in the same way as exchanging one currency for another, such as when exchanging Yen for Dollars, Pounds for Euros, or Rupees for Rand, for example.

In the realm of cryptocurrencies, exchange rates vary just like they do in the real world. Because they are still relatively new on the investment arena, one of the major contrasts between digital currencies is that their value has been rather erratic. As a result, there are frequently enormous benefits as well as equally enormous losses. When compared to the more widely used forms of money, these significant unit value swings are much more striking.

But this is also one of their fascinating qualities.

Cryptocurrency and digital currency may not be suitable for investors seeking a guaranteed return on their money. It can offer some exciting chances, yet there are always hazards associated with strong investing options. This is due to the fact that it has been demonstrated to be capable of achieving amazing amounts of development in a very short period of time. This is probable because it is still very young and, like other currencies, is likely to stabilize at considerably lower growth levels as it becomes more widely used and established. Investment now, when it's still so young, is a terrific opportunity because of this.

laying a foundational layer

It's a good idea to do as much thorough study as you can on the several cryptocurrency investing alternatives before rashly jumping on the bandwagon. It's crucial to keep a close eye on the market, as with any investment. Be ready and make a plan in advance for what you will do if the price changes, either for the better or worse. If a brokerage acts on your behalf, which is something I would suggest, there are additional tax ramifications and brokerage fees to take into account. This investment opportunity is the same as all others.

As with conventional stock brokerages, there are a lot of bitcoin exchanges. While many will appear to be fairly similar in their cost structures and the range of services they provide on the surface, it's a good idea to do some research to find out which one would best suit your needs. It is crucial to plan out exactly what you will need to do in advance in order to accomplish this. You will need to choose whether you want to trade in one or multiple cryptocurrencies, the amount of exposure you want to any given cryptocurrency, the long-term and short-term goals of your investment, the ease of use, and the amount of money you are willing to speculate.

You should consider the following factors when selecting a broker: Their costs Their guarantees The services they provide Their payment choices

How to invest in cryptocurrencies simply

These are the first actions you should take if you determine that using cryptocurrency components in your investment portfolio is a good option for you:

Ask yourself, "Can I afford to invest? Can I afford to not do it?

Choose your initial investment amount and a brokerage that trades your preferred cryptocurrency.

You can succeed in this field if you take the following actions:

1. Create an Exchange account

You need a marketplace in order to buy and/or sell things. You can get this from cryptocurrency exchanges or brokers. 'Coinbase' is currently regarded as one of the most reliable exchanges. Although this investment opportunity is completely uncontrolled as of the time of writing. Every nation in the globe is debating regulation. Because Coinbase is insured, you may feel secure knowing that your investment transactions are protected. This guarantees that you won't lose money even if your own digital security is compromised.

Additional choices include Kraken, Cex.io, ShapeShift, Poloniex, Bitstamp, CoinMama, Bitsquare, LocalBitcoin, and Gemini, among many more. There are numerous such examples; these are but a handful. Some let you buy cryptocurrencies using debit or credit cards or bank transfers, while others just let you trade one kind of coin for another.

2. Safety

Make sure you use passwords that are quite strong. Use symbols and numbers in addition to capital and lowercase letters to express yourself creatively. Use "Two-Factor Authentication" by using a program like Google Authenticator. Using a code instead of texting it is safer because text messages can be intercepted and read by crooks.

Two-factor authentication is used by Coinbase.

3. Invest in your knowledge.

Do more research, more research, more research. Your coworker's investment counsel may be sound. To conduct your own study is, however, much wiser. There are several forums where you may learn the most recent advice or learn more about a cryptocurrency that interests you. To gain a sense of the current state of the market, look at the fluctuations and trending currencies on websites like coinmarketcap.com.

4. Trading Style

Short or long term? Well, that depends entirely on you, what you are able to commit to, and what you are comfortable doing.

Margin trading, futures trading, binary options trading, prediction markets, short-selling bitcoin assets, and day trading are some short-term options to consider.

Holding on to the currency for a long time is more the focus of long-term trading. Few cryptocurrencies will be as successful as Bitcoin, but if you do your research, you should be able to identify several that will reward you with a profit if you hold onto them for an extended period of time.

5. Recognize the Market Influence of Bitcoin

Bitcoin is to the world's cryptocurrencies what the U.S. dollar is to the global economy. It is typical for Bitcoins to be used in transactions to buy other cryptocurrencies. Cross-referencing cryptocurrency charts with those of bitcoin is a good idea when trading cryptocurrencies to check for emerging patterns.

6. Value fluctuation

Try to consider the long view. You want the value to rise gradually and steadily. It requires patience for this to happen. When a coin's value changes, try not to freak out; these storms can be weathered. If you maintain your composure, there is a good chance that the value of the currency will increase once more.

Use the professionals.

Consult an expert for guidance. The counsel of experts can help you make better decisions; it may initially cost you a bit, but in the long run, it may be priceless.

8. Taxes

The IRS presently classifies cryptocurrency as a property. Therefore, it must be handled as such for your tax returns. Make sure you understand the tax implications to avoid any unpleasant surprises.

chapter summary

1. Trading cryptocurrencies is essentially the same as trading conventional fiat currencies.

2. Before making a purchase, do extensive research on all factors.

3. Select a trustworthy exchange or broker to carry out your transactions.

4. Select whether you wish to engage in long- or short-term trading.

5. Ask for professional counsel to guide you in making the right decisions.

6. Keep in mind that cryptocurrency is taxed similarly to other assets. Be mindful of your duties.

Your Quick Start Step is:

Visit the website Investopedia.com for a wealth of useful information about cryptocurrency investing.

How Do Cryptocurrencies Work?

It is crucial to describe cryptocurrencies and move beyond it to discuss its technical and financial features in order to gain a better understanding of what it is.

What is cryptocurrency?

A common understanding of cryptocurrencies is lacking. However, we can define cryptocurrency as follows for the purposes of our discussion:

Cryptography, an advanced mathematical encryption technology, is used to develop and maintain cryptocurrency, a virtual, decentralized digital currency.

Cons of cryptocurrencies

Numerous features define cryptocurrencies. Technical features, financial features, and transactional features are the three broad categories into which we might divide these characteristics.

technical aspects

Virtual - There is no actual cash in existence. It is produced using electronic codes.

Algorithmic - The nature of the codes produced is algorithmic.

Cryptic - To ensure security, the codes are encrypted. Additionally, they control the production of new coins and the validation of current currencies.

database-driven: Code records are kept in the blockchain, a type of database ledger.

Decentralized — Governmental central banks produce, distribute, and manage the majority of fiat currencies. On the other hand, open source software controls the generation and transactions of cryptocurrencies algorithmically. Peer-to-peer networks are essential for their distribution. Since they are distributed widely, no one entity can control their production.

Digital - A tangible item, such as gold, silver, etc., defines traditional fiat currency. Additionally, they are kept in vaults. Digital currencies are defined by codes rather than by any tangible items. They are stored in electronic wallets, which serve as their repository. They are transferred from the sender's digital wallet to the recipient's digital wallet in order to complete the transaction.

Adaptive scaling: Cryptocurrencies have the potential to scale up or down dynamically (automatically) to control their supply in the market, in contrast to traditional fiat currencies that are managed by interventions by monetary authorities.

Mining: Unlike traditional coins, which are created through the minting process, cryptocurrency coins are created through the mining process.

Open source - Any software developer can read the coding in the software used to mine cryptocurrencies. As a result, developers are free to design their own APIs without asking anybody else for advice or approval.

The majority of cryptocurrencies, including Bitcoin, rely on the proof-of-work approach. In this approach, the fundamental worth of the coin is obtained by solving a difficult-to-compute-but-easily-verifiable riddle. As a result, a token (coin) is produced after the problem that forms it has been solved. In place of or in addition to proof-of-work, some other cryptocurrencies employ proof-of-stake or proof-of-state.

Financial aspects

No physical control - The currency is not confined to a specific region. Both universal and global.

There is no physical authority over it, hence it is not governed by international law.

Electronically transacted - The exchange of money takes place online.

A way to measure worth - The currency is used to calculate worth using the "proof of work" (PoW) and other metrics.

Value exchange - The currency may be used as payment when exchanging products and services.

Speculative - Because the currency is driven by the market, it is subject to the dynamics of supply and demand.

Controlled supply: The majority of cryptocurrencies have a maximum number of available tokens. For instance, the 21 million maximum Bitcoin coins are anticipated to be completely mined by the year 2140. A schedule that is written in the code regulates this supply. This demonstrates transparency in the money supply so that anyone can determine the number of tokens currently in use and roughly estimate the number of tokens that will be accessible at a specific time in the future. Contrary to fiat currency, the amount in circulation with governments around the world is generally kept a secret.

No debt – Just like gold, cryptocurrencies are monetary commodities. They represent who they are. They do not reflect debts (through the IOU system) like fiat money does.

Value: A currency must stand for something in order to be valuable. Traditional currencies represented genuine gold prior to the invention of fiat money. Gold is difficult to mine and refine, making it rare. Therefore, the labor put in during this mining and refining procedure added to its basic value. Additionally, the market value was given to it by its scarcity (the laws of supply and demand). It takes a lot of effort to mine crypto currency, notably Bitcoins, and increasingly sophisticated circuitry. Due to this, bitcoins are rare.

Transactional characteristics

Secure — Only the owner of a cryptocurrency has access to the private key, whereas public keys are transmitted along with the coin transaction. Because of this, only this person can transmit cryptocurrency. The sheer size of the large numbers used to describe this complex cryptography makes it more difficult to crack.

Pseudonymous: Pseudonyms are used by cryptocurrencies so that neither transactions nor accounts can be linked to real-world identities. For instance, addresses for sending and receiving Bitcoins are chosen at random. These addresses each have about 30 characters. This address contains an encrypted identifier of the coin-holder. While you can use these randomly generated addresses to track transaction flow, you cannot use them to establish a connection to the actual identities of users. Despite being pseudonymous, the accounts are not anonymous because they are accessible to the whole public. Some cryptocurrencies, such as Monero, do, however, support both pseudonymous and anonymous features.

Permission-less - Using cryptocurrencies does not include any kind of permission-seeking structure. Software that everyone may readily download for free and use is what creates cryptocurrencies. Once the software has been downloaded, sending cryptocurrency like Bitcoin is simple. Nobody is stopping you from doing it.

Irreversible: Once a transaction has been approved, it cannot be undone.

Globally accessible quickly - Cryptocurrency transactions take place almost instantly. Networks from all across the world corroborate them in a matter of minutes. Distance is irrelevant.

How do digital currencies function?

Debit cards and cryptocurrencies both operate on the same principles. The only distinction is that public individuals rather than banks carry out bookkeeping. There isn't a single clearinghouse for them. Through blockchain, a decentralized ledger that is accessible to the public, they collaborate on bookkeeping.

Since everyone has a copy of the ledger or register, there is accountability and openness, which promotes confidence. It avoids intermediaries who would be in charge of storing the register by not being dispersed. No intermediaries, no fees for agencies.

Understanding cryptocurrency is made simpler by the ideas listed below:

Mining

General Ledger

Transactions

cryptocurrency mining

The process of confirming the algorithm of a certain token is referred to as mining. A particular token can only be classified as a cryptocurrency and added to the public ledger (blockchain) once it has been validated (checked and confirmed as real).

The individuals who perform this mining are referred to as miners. The function of miners is to safeguard the network by accepting and authenticating fresh coin issues and adding them to the public ledger. Through the use of software, a specific set of transactions' cryptographic riddles are solved, and the transactions are then added to the ledger. Coins are given to miners as payment for their labor.

Miners need specialized and advanced hardware, such as aspic chips, to conduct billions of calculations per second simply to confirm one transaction for highly mined cryptocurrencies like Bitcoin. Miners gain more cryptocurrency when they solve additional riddles. This encourages them to keep mining, assuring the security of network transactions. The underlying value of the coins is provided by the mining process. Proof of work is what this is known as.

Technology behind blockchain

A public ledger of cryptocurrency transactions is known as a blockchain. Peer-to-peer transactions are broadcast to all network users with "full-node" wallets when they are made. The cryptographic conundrum of the transaction is then attempted by miners. A few newly mined coins are awarded to the first miner who figures out the puzzle. Each transaction is a part of a block that has a secret connection to another block. As a result, when a transaction is resolved, the mysterious connection between it and the new block is revealed, and the new block is then recorded in the ledger. Between the prior block, to which the transaction belongs, and the new block revealed through the cryptic link, this link acts as a chain. It is named blockchain for this reason. The legitimacy of the ledger must first be agreed upon by all miners before it can be updated. This consensus serves as proof of labor (proof-of-work) for the miner who cracked the cryptic puzzle first.

Technically speaking, cryptocurrencies are restricted entries in a database, meaning that only particular circumstances can cause these records to change. Proof-of-work demonstrates that these requirements have been met. As a result, unlike in the old fiat currency system, a mathematical algorithm rather than a human secures the entries.

Transactions

Transferring money between two digital wallets is referred to as a transaction. A public ledger receives the transmission of this transaction. Once transmitted, information is placed in a queue for miners to confirm and verify. As a mathematical (algorithmic) verification that the transaction is coming from the owner of that specific wallet, the wallet initiating the transaction encrypts it using a cryptographic signature (encrypted electronic signature). Miners enter a cryptographic signature into the public register (ledger/blockchain) after verifying and confirming its validity.

The public code of the cryptographic signature corresponds to the user's secret password. Any cryptocurrency user can choose to download the ledger in order to have access to it. It develops into a "full node" wallet. On the other hand, they have the option of keeping their money in a third-party wallet like Coinbase.

The quantity of bitcoin represented in a given wallet's ledger (blockchain) is owned by the person who has control over its private key (private password).

The main distinction between bank notes and cryptocurrencies is that algorithms issue money and maintain ledgers, as opposed to governments and banks.

How is a cryptocurrency obtained?

Two methods exist for purchasing cryptocurrencies:

Get hold of them

(Validate their algorithm by mining them)

How Bitcoin prevents duplicate spending

Double spending occurs when a person makes multiple purchases using the same unit of currency. Compared to non-digital products, digital products are significantly simpler to replicate. Double trading is almost never done, though, given to the obscure and accounting nature of cryptocurrencies. Blockchain technology is used by cryptocurrencies to eliminate the possibility of double spending.

What makes a cryptocurrency necessary?

The following are the primary justifications for choosing cryptocurrency:

Safe hedge - Bitcoin's ability to store value is what has given it momentum. Bitcoin has emerged as the de facto benchmark for digital money. This is so because, similar to the majority of cryptocurrencies, their volume is predetermined.

Fast transaction processing is possible with cryptocurrencies because of their digital nature.

Peer-to-peer transactions are inexpensive and are used by cryptocurrencies. As a result, intermediary agents like banks and clearinghouses are removed.

Anonymous transactions are possible with cryptocurrencies.

Exists a market for trading cryptocurrencies?

Cryptocurrencies also have an exchange market, just like fiat money. On this market, cryptocurrencies are traded one for the other or against fiat money. We shall examine the top trading platforms for these markets in the next section.

Electronic cash and virtual currencies are examples of alternative currencies.

The study must begin with defining the various types of currencies in order to provide an accurate comparison. Currently, there are primarily two forms of currency used in economic systems:

Banknotes and coins that are considered legal tender

Bank deposits serve as a proxy for bank currency.

The money supply (M), which is the total of bank deposits and circulating money, is created by the union of the two types.

According to the ECB's definition, the idea of monetary aggregates can be used to describe money. These are denoted by alphanumeric abbreviations and signify stock quantities.

Banknotes, coins, and sight deposits are all included in the first aggregate, or M1. On the other hand, the M2 aggregate combines both M1 and the latter's agreed-upon deposits with a maximum maturity of two years and those redeemable with three months' notice.

The third, M3, contains repurchase agreements, money market fund holdings, and debt instruments with maturities up to two years in addition to M2.

Instead, the value of coins, bills, and liquid reserves held by central banks at the ECB are added to form the monetary base.

It is crucial to note that when we talk about "legal tender," we only refer to metallic and paper money; documentary money, like checks or credit cards, can be rejected by creditors for debts under a specific amount and is not considered legal tender.

Even though there are significant variations between the two payment systems, there is frequently confusion about the differences between e-currency and digital currencies.

In relation to electronic currencies, two categories can be distinguished:

Electronic coins that use cards

based on software electronic coins

Liquid assets are recorded by the card's microchip in the first form, whilst they are recorded on a local file that may be accessed online in the second type. Online payments, credit and debit card transactions, and bank transfers are the most popular electronic payment methods.

It is necessary to acknowledge that virtual currencies are a product of ongoing technological development in the areas of information and communication technology and electronic payment in order to complete the study.

The term "virtual currency" is defined by Legislative Decree No. 90 of May 25,

2017, as a "digital representation of value, not issued by a central bank or public authority, not necessarily linked to a legal tender, used as a means of exchange for the purchase of goods and services and transferred, traded, and stored electronically."

The TUB (Consolidated Banking Law) defines electronic money as "the electronically stored monetary value, including magnetic storage, represented by a credit towards the issuer which is issued to carry out payment operations; and which is accepted by physical and legal persons other than the issuer," which leaves no room for doubt and should make us understand the significant difference with electronic money once and for all.

It is also specified in relation to virtual currencies who the service providers are and what services they offer, i.e. "any natural or legal person who provides third parties, on a professional basis, with services functional to the use, exchange, storage, and conversion of virtual currency from, or into, legal tender currencies."

The central bank continues to oversee supply and demand, giving the relationship between electronic money and traditional money a legal foundation. The unit of account is also the same.

On the other hand, virtual currencies are subject to its swings since they are tied to actual money through an exchange rate.

Blockchain, Mining, And Ico: A New Technological Paradigm

For instance, if Bob wished to encrypt a message for Alice, he could also encrypt it with his private key and send it to Alice. Alice could then decrypt the message using only Bob's public key, allowing Alice to determine its origin.

The keys are essentially integers. A one-way elliptic function is used to extract the public key from the private key once the private key has been generated in a random manner.

The public key, which is descended from the private key as depicted in Figure 5, is a 512-bit code produced by the cryptographic algorithm ECDSA (Elliptic Curve Digital Signature Algorithm), and it is used to verify digital signatures in relation to the validity of transactions without the knowledge of the private key.

The Bitcoin address, or wallet where bitcoin is received, is then constructed from the public key using hashing methods, which ensure security.

From a technical perspective, the following will outline a Bitcoin transaction and its cryptographic ramifications.

There are multiple steps in a Bitcoin transaction between Bob (the payment) and Alice (the recipient):

A private key, or random string of digits, is created at random by Alice and stored on her computer.

The mathematical process known as the elliptic curve transforms the private key into the public key.

The public key is hashed after being encrypted. The original public key is known as the "full public key," whereas the new one is known as the "public key hash." The SHA-256 hash function is what the Bitcoin network use.

In order to represent Alice's wallet address, the public key hash is transformed into a line of up to 35 characters, such as 15VjRaDX9zpbA8LVnbrCAFzrVzN7ixHNsC.

-The first four steps take place instantly when Alice (the recipient) provides Bob the address.

Bob (the payer) decrypts the public key's hash address.

A transaction is created by the payer by defining the output (the quantity of transferred bitcoins and a "pubkey script" with the terms that render that particular bitcoins disposable, such as the requirement to use the private key to sign the transaction). In addition to the output, Bob must also provide the "signature script," which is the data the recipient must supply to confirm the transaction.

The payer sends the Bitcoins to Alice's wallet address after confirming the transaction.

Bob (the payer) sends the transaction out to the entire network, meaning that other nodes will review it for accuracy before relaying it to a miner node for confirmation.

The transaction is added to the blockchain by "miners" by placing it on a block, which the community then recognizes and accepts.

The receiver, Alice, authenticates his ownership of the transaction output by signing the "signature script" using his public and private keys.

It should be noted that the Bitcoin software entirely automates the signature procedure. Alice will now be able to use the transaction's output with Bob as an input in a subsequent transaction.

A chain of digital signatures serving as a "electronic token" is a new idea in the Bitcoin system.

The recipient's public key (the address to which to send) and the hash of the previous transaction (the condition of the BTCs' spendability, which verifies their possession) must be digitally signed by the holder of a specific amount of received BTCs before they can be transferred to the intended recipient, as shown in Figure 6.

Chain of Transactions in Figure 6

The receiver of a transaction has the ability to verify the numerous ownership changes of the digital money by going back and verifying each transaction's signatures. In fact, if even one transaction were altered, the hashes of all prior transactions would no longer match because, for instance, BTCs that were not held were spent.

Evidence of Work: Impact on Energy, Safety, and Operation

As mentioned above, mining refers to the collection of cryptographic operations carried out by miners with the intention of approving, validating, and then adding the transactions included in a block to the blockchain ledger.

Proof of work is the primary mechanism underlying mining, one of the techniques designed to reach consensus in a trustless network.

Moving on to a technical study, the proof of work (POW) algorithm is a probabilistic method for resolving the consensus issue in a decentralized network. When consensus is reached, the blocks that will be added to the chain are approved.

Each node in the network can exercise decision-making authority proportional to the processing power controlled and made available to the network in the

POW algorithm, which forms the basis of mining in the Bitcoin system.

For those taking part in the problem's solution, the likelihood that they will do so first and add a new block to the chain is directly correlated with the amount of processing power they have access to and are using to do so.

The consensus is reached by solving a cryptographic puzzle that is a computer-mathematical issue that can only be solved by a "brute force" method, or by making numerous attempts until an acceptable answer is found.

Even though these cryptographic puzzles are challenging, once a solution is found, checking the solution's accuracy is simple.

The answer to the problem is discovered by altering the data in the block in such a way that the hash computed reaches one of the solutions by having a well-defined shape termed the target. The block header information columns that make up this process are hashed, as indicated in Table 1. The generated hash must fulfill certain requirements in order to be considered legitimate.

Table 1 lists the fields that will be hashed to get the new block's hash.

In the case of Bitcoin, the hash created by synthesizing the data in Table 1 must have a specific number of consecutive and initial zeros, at least equal to those that make up the target, where the latter represents the complexity of the cryptographic problem.

We analyze the primary fields of data that must be hashed in order to solve the cryptographic challenge before explaining the last point:

Meredyth root

It represents the hash that combines every transaction in the block, including the first transaction, the "coinbase," as was previously mentioned. In order to ensure the commission margins connected with each transaction, miners have an incentive to include several transactions in the block. It is vital to note that mining a block that only contains one transaction does not make the process simpler or faster.

Bits

It indicates the target's encoding, or the degree of difficulty in solving the problem, as measured by the length of time that is needed to validate a block in comparison to when the difficulty is set to the minimal value, or 1.

The proof of work, or hash, must be obtained by combining the data in Table 1 in order for a new block to be validated and for the winning miner to reveal the answer to the network.

In other words, the goal identifies the computational effort (cpu power) necessary to crack the code and add the block.

Nonce

Literally, "number used once" refers to a parameter that is changed whenever the acquired block's hash deviates from the desired value, which enables the solution of the issue.

In actuality, the nonce is the only parameter in the information fields of the block header that can be changed in the event that the calculated hash and the intended value do not match. The nonce is typically initialized to zero and increased each time the block's hash function is calculated, until a hash value that is compatible with the given target is discovered, i.e., one that has a minimum number of leading and trailing zeros of the target.

The only way to find a block hash that is compatible with the assigned target in terms of the number of leading zeros is to modify the nonce parameter and try all possible combinations because it is impossible to predict the hash value generated by the synthesis of the data contained in the block header. In this method, as the target's needed number of beginning zeros rises, the problem's difficulty climbs exponentially.

To give you an idea, it now takes 268 attempts on average in the Bitcoin system to solve the cryptographic puzzle and "mine" a new block.

Let's use an illustration to further explain the ideas presented.

Assume that the current target is 00000011 without considering the actual length in bits of the strings that make up the information mentioned above.

For instance, if a miner hashes the block header data and comes up with a result of 0004p685, the solution is invalid since the target has 6 leading zeros while the result only has 3.

The node-miner must gradually increase the nonce parameter until the output of the cryptographic hash method begins with six zeros in order to obtain the correct answer.

Finding a hash that respects the aim can be compared to the likelihood of winning the lottery from a statistical perspective. In actuality, there is a constant probability of success for each effort at raising the nonce.

Therefore, mining is a task that must be completed through repeated tries until a workable solution is found.

In the predefined time frame of around 10 minutes, the operation and rules of mining in the Bitcoin system determine the validation and insertion into the chain of a new block of transactions.

We will now examine the "proof-of-work" method from the standpoint of security.

The proof of work makes it extremely difficult and expensive to change previous transactions that have already been added to blockchain blocks. In fact, in order to change previous transactions, a dishonest miner would need to provide a proof of work that was valid for all blocks after the one being changed.

A node-miner would need to control the vast majority (51%) of the P2P network's computer power in order to successfully change transactions that have already taken place. It is conceivable for one miner to purposefully construct the so-called "fork" of the blockchain, intended to alter previous transactions, by holding the bulk of the computer power.

In particular, the rogue miner's possession of 51% of the total computing power would enable it to solve cryptographic riddles more quickly than the other nodes in the network, enabling it to fork off a longer blockchain than the rest.

Since, in the case of a fork, the dominant or main chain ends up being the one on which more processing power is spent and hence the longer, the longer chain carried by the dishonest node would consecrate it as authoritative.

When computational power is evenly distributed among network users, proof-of-work based blockchains ensure a high level of security; otherwise, as we have seen, there is a chance of a cyberattack like the one mentioned, known as the "51% Attack." Younger blockchains with relatively little overall computer power, where it is simpler to access the absolute majority of it, definitely have a larger possibility of such an attack.

Consider a mining farm, or a business that owns a large number of hardware devices to perform the activity of mining, even though it will be covered in the parts that follow. In this way, this business, as opposed to an independent miner who owns only one piece of hardware, may benefit from economies of scale and make significant profits.

When two node-miners simultaneously discover two correct, but different, answers to the cryptographic conundrum to be solved, that is a special case that needs to be examined. As a result, the chain would split, and for a brief moment, there would be two legitimate, concurrent versions of the blockchain. The establishment of a consensus in this situation would be made possible by Bitcoin's proof of work, determining which of the two versions is the dominant chain.

Technically, in the case of a fork, each node chooses one of the two blockchains at random and uses it as the foundation for building new blocks in the future. This establishes a division of the network's computational capacity between the two competing blockchains, establishing the chain that has been extended more swiftly, adding the next block first, as the official chain because more of the system's computational power has been employed on it.

If determined to be genuine (no duplicate spending), the transactions found in the "orphans" blocks of the shortest supply chain will be added to the queue and then included in the block that will be connected to the main blockchain. No miner will use the shorter chain, known as orphan, as a foundation for adding additional transaction blocks. This is because of game theory, specifically because each player (miner) is convinced that it is not profitable to maintain the shorter blockchain because it is not the official version and they would not be able to receive rewards and commissions. The miner who first puts the following block in the chain during the competitive process only receives the latter in the Bitcoin protocol after 100 confirmations, or after the addition of 100 additional blocks to the one he entered. Due to the possibility of forks, it is necessary to wait for the addition of a significant number of succeeding blocks to the block in which the transaction we are considering is included before considering a transaction to be executed and ensure that it won't be reversed in the event of a fork.

In fact, it is shown that the likelihood that a block of transactions will be removed due to a chain bifurcation decreases exponentially with each block that is added. This likelihood is thought to be nearly negligible in the Bitcoin network after adding around six blocks to the chain, taking the transaction into account.

The mining activity accomplished with the proof of work mechanism indicates a method of reaching consensus in a trustless network at this point, it looks clearer and more understandable. We then examine the energy implications of mining activity.

The proof-of-work algorithm's heavy reliance on energy resources to function is undoubtedly its major flaw. In fact, many experts believe that the high energy cost associated with solving the cryptographic puzzles that guarantee blockchain security is a flaw that could restrict the scalability of proof-of-work-based blockchains.

This restriction served as the impetus for the creation of new, more energy-efficient algorithms that are employed in the consensus procedure and are covered in the following two sections of this chapter.

Now that the technique for enabling the answer to the cryptographic conundrum—the conundrum on which the consensus process in the blockchain is based—is known, the meaning of the phrase "proof of work" is unquestionably clearer. According to this reasoning, consensus is progressive because the nodes, to whom the miner who initially found the answer communicates it, confirm that the block does not contain any transactions that conflict with one another and further confirm it by using the block's hash to create the subsequent block, thereby extending the chain.

Alternative approach: Proof of Stake (possible problems)

As explained in the preceding section, the proof of stake algorithm was created as an alternative to the energy-inefficient proof of work technique of reaching consensus in the blockchain.

Through the use of this technique, the network's participants (or nodes) vote in order to obtain a consensus.

Each node in the blockchain is granted the ability to vote merely by holding bitcoin, and the number of votes that may be cast is inversely correlated with the amount of cryptocurrency held.

Proof-of-stake algorithms are preferable to proof-of-work algorithms because they require less time to produce blocks and use less energy, which is a disadvantage of the former. This is because a vote requires a lot less processing power than solving cryptographic puzzles, can be completed faster, and guarantees more effective performance.

On the other side, there is a chance of a system attack of the "51% attack" type even with this alternative approach of reaching shared consensus.

However, it should be noted that compared to a blockchain that uses proof of work, this kind of attack is considerably less likely.

In fact, the cost of the assault would be high in a proof of stake system. A node would need to own the majority of the available cryptocurrency in order to put it into action.

In contrast to the proof-of-work criterion, where controlling 51% of the network's computing power is enough to attack the system, this condition is unquestionably far more challenging to fulfill. However, even if a node ends up controlling more than half of all cryptocurrency in use, the likelihood of it attacking the network is still extremely slim because it would be taking on the most of the risk.

The cyberattack may even cause the network to collapse and erode trust in the system, which would have a highly negative impact on the price of cryptocurrencies.

Since he controls the majority of the available currency, the attacker (dishonest node) would sustain the most harm if this were to occur.

We now examine the problems with proof-of-stake algorithms.

In actuality, they are considerably more difficult to construct and deploy than proof-of-work.

Despite this problem, the punishment of nodes who engage in dishonest behavior during the consensus process is the main problem.

Using a bifurcation of the blockchain as an example, the optimum course of action is for each node to vote for both versions of the chain because there is no cost to taking part in the vote.

As a result, there is a blocking situation in which consensus cannot be reached since neither version of the blockchain will be accepted as the official/main version.

It's critical to keep in mind that this cannot happen in a proof-of-work blockchain because each node will select only one of the two chains and use its own financial resources (hardware purchase) to solve the cryptographic issues associated with the selected chain. Then, each node-minor would concentrate its computational resources on the chain that it thought had a greater chance of succeeding as the dominant chain.

Variety of Knots

Any participant in the blockchain peer-to-peer network, or computer connected to the network, has been referred to as a "node" throughout the discussion up to this point. Following our discussion of the technology's key ideas, we can now go on to comparing and contrasting the many nodes—or network participants—that make up the network. There are only three distinct categories of nodes:

Node alone Mining

Whole Node

Node SPV

By resolving computational issues in mathematics and information science, the initial group of nodes actively contributes to the formation of transaction blocks. The mining nodes that reach a consensus more quickly, validating a block to be added to the chain, support the development of the network and are subsequently rewarded with cryptocurrency units in accordance with a well-established incentive structure. For instance, the mining incentive also serves as the means of coin generation in the Bitcoin system, as was already mentioned.

Similar to mining-only nodes, full nodes maintain the entire blockchain ledger, starting with the genesis block (also known as the first block) and ending with the most recent block added to the chain, before the block they are currently working on is validated. They are notified each time a transaction is started so that it can spread across the network until it reaches the miners who, by including it in the block, confirm it. They maintain a history of the blocks that the miners have solved.

SPV nodes, or "Simplified Payment Verification" nodes, are the third kind. The block header and the Merkle root are the only two parts of the blockchain record that this type of node, also known as a light node, retains. An SPV node will only commit to verifying its own transactions by securing these pieces, not all transactions launched in the network. For a transaction to be approved in the Bitcoin system and transmitted throughout the network, it must be near a complete node and not be incompatible with the history displayed by the blockchain. The transactions are then forwarded to the miners by the full nodes so that they can finally put them into the blockchain and confirm them.

Mine in a solo, pool, or cloud mode.

There are 3 basic methods for performing the mining activity, which verifies blocks of transactions before they are added to the blockchain:

Solo-Mining

when each miner works alone with the intention of earning money from the rewards connected with validating blocks and the transaction fees associated with them.

For this particular mode to hold a high level of processing power and compete in the competitive mining mechanism, large individual hardware investments are needed. It is obvious that increased controlled processing power is correlated with a higher likelihood of cracking cryptographic riddles and adding new blocks to the chain, increasing earnings. Nevertheless, this technique does not ensure ongoing cash flows.

Pool-Mining

As opposed to the previously described individual mining, this process can be carried out in a group setting, for instance by joining a mining pool. In this setting, multiple participants contribute their computing power, and the profits are divided according to the contribution made, in terms of computational power. This mode, in contrast to the first, enables mining even without the use of powerful technology and provides steady revenue flows over time, even if only in tiny amounts.

Cloud-Mining

There are various businesses, referred to as Mining Farms, that frequently let the leasing of a specific quantity of processing power of their hardware devices for a specific duration against a subscription. As a result, pool mining enables you to engage in mining activities even without the necessary hardware instruments, as well as solving the issues associated with the upkeep and deployment of such equipment.

Profits are thus in line with the contribution provided according to the sort of contract that was signed.

Chapter 1: Money Talks

You ought to have a solid understanding of the fundamentals of money before we get into cryptocurrency. Keep in mind that bitcoins are a type of payment. You will be able to appreciate money more and comprehend its genuine nature if you learn about and comprehend its nature, particularly its attributes.

What is currency?

People often use money to symbolize the worth of other things.

As an example, you provided cash in exchange for a book. The seller can buy something valuable from other merchants with the money they received.

If we go back in time, we can see that money as we know it today wasn't always the main way people made purchases. Gold, shells, salt, wheat, and other valuable items were once commonly utilized as a form of exchange. If the general population continues to believe in a specific form of exchange, it will continue to represent value and people will continue to be able to use it to their advantage in the future.

People eventually realized that employing materials like gold, shells, salt, or wheat as a medium may be highly taxing. Can you imagine purchasing your food today with wheat or salt? What if you need to buy food for a month? How much wheat are you taking to the shop, do you think? Can you imagine yourself, as the grocery store owner, measuring all that wheat for which your customer has paid? What happens if it rains and you don't have a car? Do you see the picture now?

People had to find a more workable and practical solution because it was too inconvenient, which led to the invention of paper money.

They will first issue you certificates or bills for the value of the gold you put when you visit the bank or government facility to receive your gold bars for storage. If you own gold bars worth $500, for instance, the government or the bank will seize the gold and issue a paper certificate (or banknotes) for $500 in exchange. It would make sense because carrying cash about would be simpler than carrying gold bars.

All you'd need to do to get your gold bars back is pay $500 in certificates or notes. That's straightforward and useful.

Previously, a system known as the Gold Standard underpinned the value of the US dollar and was based on gold. But gradually, the macroeconomy seized control and adjustments were made. The US dollar was regarded as the world's reserve currency, and Americans as well as the rest of the world were forced to switch their allegiance from gold to the federal government.

Fiat, or paper money, was created in this way.

Fiat Currency

The Latin phrase "by decree" is called "fiat." Paper money and other fiat currencies only have value because the government declares they do. Fiat money was also known as "legal tender," which meant that it should be accepted as payment for goods and services in any country where it is issued.

This is the currency in use right now.

The power to issue money and manage the money supply belongs to a single, centralized entity. The Federal Reserve, for instance, serves as the ultimate authority for the US dollar. The US dollar has a limitless supply, but the Federal Reserve has the ability and tools to print more of them if necessary.

The basic tenet of supply and demand is that when the quantity of an item increases, its value decreases, presuming that the demand for that item remains constant. On the other hand, if the supply is reduced and the demand for the good remains constant, its value will rise.

The market will be oversaturated with cash if the Federal Reserve or any other monetary authority prints more, making it useless for making purchases of goods and services.

Therefore, if you see that the cost of goods and services is rising, it wasn't because the goods themselves cost more; rather, it was due to the value of the currency.

Money Digitization

Digital money was made possible by the invention of fiat money. The increased usage of the internet and technological advancements make digitizing money simpler. This is merely adapting to contemporary circumstances in which various payment methods have been developed.

Cash payments have long been replaced by credit cards. Emerging trends like e-wallets and fund transfers have established themselves as trusted methods of payment. Paying in cash has become unusual, and in some circumstances suspicious, just in the US.

The repercussions are severe. One of them is the steady fall in the amount of real money in circulation in the majority of the world's largest financial and economic systems.

Then, how does digital currency operate? How can money be doubly spent avoided?

The majority of financial organizations use centralization to overcome this problem. Under a certain system, there would only be one entity responsible for keeping track of financial transactions in order to identify owners and their respective ownership stakes. Every person who does business using that system has a unique account, which corresponds to a distinct ledger where all of their transactions and balances are kept track of.

Everyone has faith in the financial institutions' computer systems to maintain accurate records, and they will have faith in their own computer systems as well. A ledger that is kept in a solitary computer system or network is the foundation for the centralization of records. Prior to the invention of the blockchain, numerous attempts to develop substitute digital payment methods failed due to a crucial problem: how to avoid double-spending without a central authority.

Keeping records in a centralized system still makes sense today since it is effective.

System of Centralized Money

There will always be issues that need to be resolved right away if we give someone or a group of individuals total command and control over something.

Significant obstacles include control, poor management, and corruption.

It will be required by law for central banks and other monetary authorities, such as the Federal Reserve, to print money and create value. In the case of the Federal Reserve, these will have total influence over how value is created and destroyed both within their own nations and globally.

Corruption

The saying goes, "Absolute power corrupts absolutely." One incident where this happened included a financial institution, where staff members were instructed to register false bank and credit card accounts in an effort to boost sales and, ultimately, net profits for a number of years.

Mismanagement

Mismanagement in business refers to a worker failing to perform or behave as expected by their employer (the business owner). Mismanagement in monetary authorities occurs when the government goes against the interests of its citizens. As an illustration, consider how the U.S. monetary authorities permitted sizable financial organizations to provide credit-linked notes or financial derivatives with mortgages that carried high default risks but were rated as investment grade by dishonest rating agencies. This is due to the factors that led to the American financial system's impending collapse in 2008. In order to save the largest financial firms at the time, the Federal Reserve intervened by utilizing public funds against the wishes of the general population.

The production of fresh money without taking into account its deflationary repercussions is another example of poor management. Recall that we previously stated that printing more money would overwhelm the financial system, which might cause the value of a particular currency to decline (law of supply and demand). The Venezuelan government experienced this; they printed too much money, rendering their currency worthless, to the point where their citizens started valuing their money by weight rather than quantity.

Control

The worst-case scenario is that the government freezes people's bank accounts, prohibiting them from accessing their own money. The government has complete authority over the money of its citizens. Additionally, having cash on hand does not ensure that the government won't be able to prevent you from utilizing it. By revokeing its legal tender status, your government might still prevent you from utilizing your own money. In the past, this occurred in India.

Silver and gold

Gold and silver are actual forms of currency, not just investments! Keep in mind that governmental currencies are merely currencies, just like the fiat currency, and that currencies are not the same as money.

How so? First off, the money is legal tender, and the government, not the people, decides what it is worth.

Second, legitimate money possesses qualities that most government-issued currencies, such as the US dollar or the European pound, do not. The following are the seven qualities of "legit money":

The ease of usage is the main deterrent to using lead or copper as money.

Durability is the reason that people no longer use salt and wheat as currency.

Paintings and other works of art cannot be used as currency due to the concept of divisibility.

The reason why real estate cannot be used to purchase goods or services is consistency in value

The concept of intrinsic value explains why paper money lacks true value.

Rocks or iron cannot be used as currency due to a limited supply.

Reputation for acceptability

Only the metals gold and silver can genuinely meet the aforementioned qualities when they are thoroughly examined. Consider the worth of financial assets like bonds, equities, or real estate; due to their varying prices, it is not constant. Silver and gold have enduring value; their prices never change. You can assert that currencies are not genuine money even more strongly if you take into account the fact that only gold and silver have maintained a high value from the dawn of civilization.

Can their worth be changed?

Now let's examine gold. Price manipulation refers to any deliberate attempt to influence the price of gold.

This can occur on significant financial markets when gold traders can consciously attempt to use derivatives and other specialized financial instruments to try and influence gold prices. The real values of gold may be subject to short-term fluctuations at the hands of these traders, but this doesn't seem to be the case over the long run.

Manipulation is defined by the United States Securities and Exchange Commission as an intentional conduct intended to deceive investors by artificially influencing or dominating the market for a certain asset. This includes manipulating quotes and making a lot of trades to give the impression that there is a high demand for a certain item in order to manipulate market prices in their (traders') favor. Price suppression, or manipulating prices downward, is the sole sort of manipulation being utilized to influence the price of gold.

Is it true that gold (and silver) prices are being manipulated? The majority of gold traders would claim that it was manipulable. Could this possibly be true?

There are a number of defenses for this assertion.

One is that these precious metals' prices are in fact managed by central banks. Another is that avaricious private commercial bankers are rigging the market through high-volume trading, derivative instruments (including short sales and futures contracts), and artificially low and diminishing demand for gold (and silver).

Due to prior instances of controlling gold prices, such as when the government set gold prices for decades or the London Gold Pool hid its prices, these arguments may appear reasonable. The punishment of financial institutions for manipulating gold prices is likewise rather uncommon.

The answer to the issue, however, becomes rather obvious if you delve into the lengthy price histories of both gold and silver: no, the prices of gold and silver cannot be manipulated. There will never be strong evidence to support the existence of price suppression or manipulation.

How Do Digital Currencies Function?

The basis of cryptocurrencies is block chains, a decentralized public database that keeps track of all transactions and is updated by currency owners. The practice of "mining," which entails employing computer power to solve challenging mathematical problems, produces bitcoin units. The option exists for users to purchase the currencies from brokers, keep them in digital wallets, and then use them.

Holders of cryptocurrencies don't actually possess anything. You hold the secret to moving information or units of measurement between individuals without the help of a reliable middleman.

Even though Bit coin has been around since 2009, block chain technology and its financial applications are still in their infancy, and more applications are anticipated in the future. Future trading of bonds, stocks, and other financial assets may be possible with this technology.

The types of cryptocurrencies are numerous. The most popular ones consist of:

Bitcoin: As the first cryptocurrency and currently the most well-known, Bitcoin was created in 2009. The invention of the currency is credited to an individual or group, whose specific identity is still a mystery and who is often only known by the alias Satoshi Nakamoto.

Ether (ETH), often known as Ethereum, is a digital currency used on the block chain platform Ethereum, which was launched in 2015. After Bit coin, it is the most widely used cryptocurrency.

Although Litecoin has created new technologies more swiftly, allowing for speedier payments and more transaction-enabling processes, Bit coin is most comparable to Litecoin.

A distributed ledger system called Ripple was created in 2012. Ripple can be used to trace transactions using currencies other than bitcoin. The business that founded it has collaborated with numerous banks and financial organizations.

Non-Bitcoin cryptocurrencies are generally referred to as "altcoins" to set them apart from the original.

Techniques for obtaining cryptocurrencies

What is the safest way to purchase cryptocurrencies? Typically, there are three steps. Which are:

Selecting a platform is the first step.

Choosing the platform is the first step. Generally speaking, you have the option of selecting a conventional broker or one of a specific crypto currency exchange's regular brokers. These are online brokers that allow customers to purchase and sell cryptocurrencies as well as stocks, bonds, ETFs, and other types of financial assets. Even while they typically offer fewer crypto capabilities, certain platforms have reduced trading costs. You have a variety of options for crypto currency exchanges, and they all offer services like access to various digital assets, wallet storage, alternative interest-bearing account options, and more. Asset-based fees are common on exchanges. When contrasting various platforms, take into account the prices, security features, storage and withdrawal possibilities, and any instructional resources that might be accessible.

The second step is to fund your account.

Funding your account so you may start trading comes after selecting your trading platform. Although it differs per platform, the majority of cryptocurrency exchanges let users buy cryptocurrency with fiat (i.e., government-issued) money like the US Dollar, the British Pound, or the Euro using their debit or credit cards. It is not recommended to use a credit card to purchase cryptocurrencies, and some exchanges do not accept them. Furthermore, a lot of credit card providers forbid bitcoin transactions. Due to the extreme volatility of the market and the possibility of hefty credit card transaction fees, some assets shouldn't be purchased using cryptocurrencies.

Additionally, certain systems might handle wire transfers and ACH transactions. Depending on the platform, different withdrawal and deposit processing times and accepted payment methods apply. Deposits settle in a variety of times depending on the type of payment.

Cost is an important consideration. These include potential transaction fees for deposits and withdrawals as well as trading costs. Do your homework in advance because fees will vary depending on the platform and payment choice.

Step 3: Buying something

To place an order, you can use the web or mobile interfaces provided by your brokerage or exchange. By clicking "buy," selecting an order type, providing the necessary quantity, and then submitting the order, you can purchase bitcoin assets. The "sell" orders are processed using the same method. The options for investing in cryptocurrency are increasingly varied. These include cryptocurrency buying, selling, and storage options offered via online payment systems like PayPal, Cash App, and Venmo.

The following platforms are also available for investing:

Bitcoin-holding trusts: A standard brokerage account can be used to purchase shares of trusts that contain bitcoins. These products give regular investors access to cryptocurrencies via the stock market. Mutual funds and exchange-traded funds (ETFs) for Bitcoin can be purchased. Through block chain companies that are experts in the technology that underpins cryptocurrencies and cryptocurrency transactions, it is also possible to invest in cryptocurrencies indirectly through block chain stocks or ETFs. Investing in exchange-traded funds (ETFs) or stock of businesses that utilise blockchain technology is another option. The ideal option for you will depend on your risk tolerance and investing objectives.

Four recommendations for secure bitcoin investments

Consumer Reports states that all investments involve risk, but some professionals believe that bitcoin is one of the riskier investing options currently accessible. If you intend to invest in cryptocurrencies, the following guidance may help you make sensible choices.

research partnerships

Before making an investment, research bitcoin exchangers. There are reportedly around 500 exchanges available. Do your homework, study reviews, and talk to more experienced investors before continuing.

Learn how to store your digital cash safely:

You must keep the bitcoin you purchase. It may be stored on an exchange or in a digital wallet. There are many distinct sorts of wallets, and each has benefits, technological requirements, and security requirements. Similar to exchanges, you should examine your storage choices before making an investment.

Diversify your investments:

Diversification is a key component of any smart investment strategy, including cryptocurrency investments. For instance, just because you know what Bitcoin is, don't invest all of your money in it. There are several possibilities, and it is advisable to spread your investment over different currencies.

Anticipate turbulence:

Because of the volatility of the bitcoin market, be prepared for ups and downs. You'll observe large price fluctuations. If you can't handle cryptocurrency because of your financial condition or mental health, it might not be a good choice for you.

Although cryptocurrency is very trendy right now, keep in mind that it is still very speculative and in its early stages. Be prepared because investing in anything new will present challenges. If you intend to take part, do your study and invest just a little bit of money.

How to safeguard cryptocurrency

After purchasing cryptocurrency, you must protect it effectively from theft and hackers. Your coins' private keys are frequently kept safely in crypto wallets, which can be either online programs or pieces of physical hardware. You can store money there more easily if an exchange offers wallet services. Not all brokers or exchanges, nevertheless, promptly offer you wallet services.

You have a variety of wallet providers to pick from. "Hot wallet" and "cold wallet" are phrases we use:

Hot wallet holding: "Hot wallets" are a type of cryptocurrency storage that encrypts the private keys to your holdings using internet software.

Keeping cold wallets in storage Cold wallets (also known as hardware wallets) employ offline electrical devices to store your private keys as opposed to hot wallets, which do so using online computers. Although cold wallets can occasionally do so, hot wallets typically don't.

What Products Can You Buy Using Cryptocurrencies?

When it was initially created, Bitcoin was intended to be a tool for conducting everyday commerce, making it simple to purchase everything from a cup of coffee to a computer or even pricey things like real estate. Even if more organizations are embracing cryptocurrencies, significant transactions using them are still rather rare, so that hasn't entirely happened yet. Even said, using bitcoin enables you to purchase a wide range of things through e-commerce websites. Here are several examples:

Technology and online stores: Cryptocurrencies are accepted by a variety of businesses that sell tech products online, including newegg.com, AT&T, and Microsoft. Overstock was one of the first online merchants to accept

Bit money. Additionally, Shopify, Rakuten, and Home Depot accept them.

Few high-end retailers accept bitcoin as payment for luxury products. For instance, the online luxury retailer Bitdials sells upmarket watches like Rolex, Patek Philippe, and others for Bit money.

Automobiles: A small number of auto businesses, from high-end luxury dealers to mass-market manufacturers, currently accept cryptocurrencies as payment.

Insurance: Swiss corporation AXA stated in April 2021 that it has begun taking Bitcoin as payment for all of its insurance lines, with the exception of life insurance (owing to legal restrictions). Premier Shield Insurance offers house and car insurance coverage in the US and also accepts bitcoin for premium payments. If you want to spend Bitcoin at a store that doesn't take it directly, use a bitcoin debit card, like BitPay in the US.

How To Understand Cryptocurrencies

It's crucial for folks to understand basic monetary ideas and how money functions in order to learn about cryptocurrencies. You won't be able to buy, sell, or exchange it before that.

Computers that are a member of the decentralized networks are known as nodes in the bitcoin world. Any computer that is capable of handling complex computations and has the necessary software installed can function as a node. It maintains all transaction records and administers the blockchain software. By installing the blockchain application on your computer, you can set up a node.

The blockchain

Blockchain verifies digital currency. Blockchains are essentially collections of connected records. There are three parts to each block of records: a hashpointer, a timestamp, and transaction information. Following their passage through the nodes, all messages sent by the sender are documented in the Blockchain.

An example of a shared data set is a blockchain, which differs from a common data set in that it stores data in blocks that are subsequently linked together using cryptography.

Every time fresh information is received, a new block is created. When the block is filled with data, it is bonded to the previous block, tying the data together in a sequential fashion.

Although several types of data can be stored on a blockchain, up until now the most well-known application has been as a transactional record.

Since decentralized blockchains are immutable, the data entered on them must be irreversible. This implies that transactions involving Bitcoin are always recorded and visible to everyone.

Blockchain and bitcoin are two distinct concepts that are frequently used interchangeably. The fact that the Bitcoin blockchain was the first cryptocurrency-specific blockchain to be introduced explains why the two have been combined.

Visit the following website to learn more about blockchain and how it functions: https://www.investopedia.com/terms/b/blockchain.asp

The transaction and the transaction value

Electronic crypto wallets are used to send and receive transactions, which are digitally signed for security.

Any cryptocurrency transaction must take into account these three things:

the sum, which is also referred to as the transactional value, the input, and the output

An output is an address to which the money is transferred, whereas an input is the place where the amount is stored and from which it is sent. Money can be sent from more than one input to more than one output since a wallet can have a number of input addresses. Additionally, each transaction includes a major form with an information hoarding section that lets you permanently save information on the blockchain.

The transactions cannot be changed or undone because doing so would require redoing all the blocks, which is a difficult procedure to carry out. Different currencies and blockchains have different processing times for transactions.

Money pouches

Wallets today differ from the ones I used to keep my money in. Email wallets and other wallets are used to save cryptocurrency coins. The addresses you just used to receive and spend the cryptocurrency are essentially saved in the cryptocurrency wallets along with the coins itself. There are numerous ways to access the money stored in the wallet. Keys can be kept in the wallet via a paper wallet, a hardware wallet, a digital wallet, or an exchange.

Cryptocurrency must be securely stored in wallets after purchase. Cryptocurrency experts advise against exchanging cryptocurrency because it is safer to save it in hardware or software.

The hardware wallet is frequently referred to as the Cold Water Storage and the software wallet as the Hot Wallet Storage.

- Coins

The image that comes to mind when we think of coins is of the physical coins that we use every day to make purchases. The units of currency used in cryptocurrencies are strings of bits, or the ones and zeros of binary computer language. It functions essentially as an impenetrable cryptographic messaging system. To be more precise, it refers to the value you receive while buying and selling cryptocurrencies. Bitcoin is the most prevalent example of a crypto currency.

Exchange of

Exchange is one of the most crucial components of cryptocurrencies.

Businesses that enable customers to trade cryptocurrencies are known as cryptocurrency exchanges. Exchanges either convert cryptocurrency into cards or deliver it to ATMs so that consumers can withdraw cash. While some exchanges enable peer to peer trading of cryptocurrencies, others merely store them. The top exchanges of 2022 are shown below:

Coinbase, Crypto.com, Binanace, Cash App, Bit Mart, and Mining are just a few examples.

Unlike traditional currency, which is printed, cryptocurrency exists. By competing with one another, computers all over the world "mine" for coins. The process of discovering new blocks, validating exchanges, and adding them to the blockchain is known as crypto mining.The successful miner is given the option to add fresh exchange data to each new block that is discovered.

Winning miners receive a free freshly created coin called as a "block reward" in exchange for investing time and resources to carrying out this task, as well as any costs associated with exchanges they store in the new blocks.

Giving new coins to miners is intended to allow the coin to circulate.

How do you purchase cryptocurrencies?

There are only three easy actions you need to take to purchase bitcoin, which are covered below:

1- Initial Step

Finding and choosing a platform to purchase, sell, or invest in cryptocurrencies is the first step. In general, there are two types of platforms: traditional brokers and cryptocurrency exchanges. You can purchase and sell cryptocurrencies as well as other financial assets like bonds, equities, ETFs, and NFTs using regular brokers. Traditional brokers offer less cryptocurrency capabilities in comparison, but they can be an excellent starting point for new users. Exchanges for cryptocurrencies offer a variety of services, such as wallets, accounts, and various kinds of cryptocurrency. These exchanges also occasionally levy an asset-based fee. \

2- Next Step

Finding your account to start trading cryptocurrencies is the next step after choosing the platform. You can buy coins or tokens on many cryptocurrency exchanges using dollars, euros, or any other form of currency you may already have in your possession. Credit card payment is not recommended because cryptocurrency is quite volatile and may result in debt. Mining coins and using the proceeds to purchase new cryptocurrencies is a secure solution.

The Foundations of Bitcoin

The introduction of the bitcoin as a legitimate, widely used currency has started sparking intense discussion about the "future" of the global economy, making it one of the potentially most disruptive, exciting, and divisive new developments in global economics. Having said that, many people simply haven't been satisfied with this new, online-only financial resource, in large part because of its exclusion from the "real" world.

The invention of Bitcoin can be dated to 2008, when 'Satoshi Nakamoto,' a pseudonym used by the currency's inventor, introduced his 'peer-to-peer' currency to the world. As opposed to central government authentication, BitCoin is defined as a "cryptocurrency," or a form of money that is created and transferred using a variety of cryptographic tools. The Bitcoin is intended to be "independent" from national interests and interactions, developing "worth" as a result of its sovereignty and resistance to inflation.

Virtual currencies like bitcoins have several characteristics in common with traditional money. They are the first currency without a central issue thanks to their robust cryptography and peer-to-peer network. Although they are not physical objects, bitcoins function virtually in the same way.

Initially, bitcoins were traded on bitcointalk forums, becoming the property of enthusiasts who think that cryptographic protocols might spur political and social change. This group of enthusiasts is known as the cypherphunk community.

Two years later, bitcoin has been embraced by a larger and larger section of the world's population, allowing entrepreneurs to create active trading platforms for the currency.

There are presently many platforms that permit intra-currency trading for anyone interested in using bitcoin as a means of international exchange. The bigger platforms include Kraken, Mt. Gox, VirWox, and Interango. Each of these exchange vehicles offers a distinctive range of services and maneuvers. Due to both the volatile nature of the currency and the absence of a comprehensive regulatory infrastructure for the exchanges, security is extremely important in bitcoin trading. Having said that, these currency exchange software platforms draw a large number of users, the majority of whom can conduct transactions without incident.

The value of Bitcoin is typically somewhat unstable, in large part because it is a popular tool for people transacting illegal services who want to remain anonymous. Recent government-backed Bitcoin seizures have caused the value of the currency to fluctuate greatly. Having said that, during the past two years, the per-unit value of bitcoin has increased astronomically.

Bitcoin is a type of currency that only exists in the digital world. The technology was developed by a person going unnoticed by using the name Satoshi Nakamoto. The creator(s) of the system have never been identified, maintaining an anonymous status, to this day.

As there are no physical representations for the cryptocurrency, bitcoins are not printed like traditional currencies; instead, they are created by users and several businesses through a process known as mining. This is where specialized software provides solutions to mathematical puzzles in exchange for virtual money.

It is controlled by a user utilizing electronic devices, which also act as a conduit for concluding transactions with the aid of numerous platforms. It is also maintained and secured through the use of virtual walls.

Characteristics of Bitcoin

Bitcoin has the characteristics of conventional currencies, such as buying power and making investments using online trading tools. It functions similarly to conventional money, with the exception that it is limited to the digital world.

One of its distinctive qualities that cannot be matched by fiat currency is that it is decimalized. The fact that the money is not controlled by a governmental body or an institution implies that users have full ownership of their bitcoins because it cannot be managed by these entities.

More importantly, transactions take place using Bitcoin addresses, which are unrelated to any names, addresses, or other personal information requested by conventional payment systems.

Every single Bitcoin transaction is recorded on a public ledger known as the "blockchain," which anybody may see. If a user uses a publicly accessible address, their information is shared for everyone to see, but not with their personal information, of course.

Unlike conventional banks that request a great deal of information and may put their customers in danger due to the frauds and schemes involving the system, accounts are simple to create.

Additionally, the quantity of Bitcoin transaction fees will always be small. Apart from processing finishing in almost real-time, no fees are known to be big enough to put a debit on someone's account.

Uses of Bitcoin Aside from its ability to be used to purchase goods and services, one of its well-known applications includes its use for a variety of investment vehicles. This includes trading on Forex, Bitcoin, and binary options platforms. Additionally, businesses provide services that revolve on Bitcoin as currency.

Clearly, Bitcoin is just as flexible as conventional legal monies. With its ease of use and profit-making capabilities, its introduction offers every individual new beneficial opportunities.

The advantages of trading currencies

There are several reasons why you should think about purchasing the currency. Some of these motives include:

The ease of entry: There are almost no barriers to entry into the Bitcoin market, in contrast to the stock market and other trading channels. All you have to do is identify a seller from whom you can purchase. If you're interested in selling, find a buyer, and you're good to go.

• International: You can trade currency in any region of the world. This implies that a person in China can buy or sell Bitcoin to a person in Africa or anywhere else. This makes the currency significant because it isn't impacted by the economy of a single nation.

It is flammable: Like the other currencies traded on foreign exchange markets, Bitcoin is highly liquid. This indicates that it quickly changes its price in response to minor changes in the economy. Take advantage of the adjustments to maximize your profits.

▪ 24/7 shipping: Unlike the stock market, which is open just during business hours, bitcoin trading is open 24/7. The trading restrictions are only on you, not on time.

How to obtain Bitcoins

There are many ways to obtain the currency if you are interested in entering the market. Some examples of the methods you can utilize are:

• Purchasing a change: You must enter the marketplace in order to locate those looking to sell the currency here. You should choose a trustworthy seller and place an order.

• Transfers: You could also borrow bitcoin from a friend. Here, a buddy must use an app that is installed on a computer or phone to transfer you the money.

The mining industry: This is the conventional method of obtaining the coins. This strategy involves using a computer to solve challenging arithmetic problems. You receive the coins after finishing a puzzle successfully. Despite being free, this method is typically time-consuming.

Consider Investing. Think Of Bitcoin This Way

Just what is Bitcoin?

If you are here, then you are aware of Bitcoin. It has been one of the most often reported news stories over the past year or two, whether as a get-rich-quick scheme, the end of banking, the emergence of really international currency, the end of the world, or a technology that has improved the world. What is Bitcoin, though?

In a nutshell, you might say that Bitcoin is the first decentralized payment system used for online transactions, but it will probably be helpful to delve a little further.

In general, we all understand what "money" is and what it is used for. The most significant problem with money use prior to Bitcoin is that it was centralized and controlled by one system, the centralized banking system. An unidentified creator going by the pseudonym "Satoshi Nakamoto" invested in Bitcoin in 2008 or 2009 to bring decentralization to money on a worldwide scale. The idea is that money would become more democratic and equally available to everyone if it could be traded across international borders without difficulty or fees and that checks and balances would be distributed throughout the entire world rather than just on the books of private corporations or governments.

How was Bitcoin created?

The idea of Bitcoin and cryptocurrency in general was first introduced in 2009 by an unidentified researcher named Satoshi. It was created to address the problem of centralization in the use of money that depended on banks and computers, a problem that many computer scientists weren't happy with. Since the late 1990s, attempts to achieve decency have been made without success, so when Satoshi published a paper in 2008 offering a solution, it was warmly received. Today, Bitcoin has established itself as a well-known cryptocurrency among internet users and has given rise to thousands of "altcoins" (cryptocurrencies that are not Bitcoin).

How is Bitcoin created?

Bitcoin is created using a process known as mining. Similar to how gold is mined from the earth and paper money is created through printing, bitcoin is created through "mining." Mining is employing computers to solve complex mathematical puzzles with blocks and adding the solutions to a public ledger. When it first started, all you needed to mine was a basic CPU (like the one in your home computer), but today you'll need specialized hardware, including high-end Graphics Processing Units (GPUs), in order to extract Bitcoin.

How should I invest?

You must first open an account with a trading platform and generate a wallet; you can find several examples by searching Google for "Bitcoin trading platforms"; these platforms typically have names that include "coin" or "market." You join one of these platforms, click on the exchanges, then click on cryptocurrency to select your desired currencies. You should be sure to pay close attention to all of the extremely crucial indications on each platform before making an investment because there are many of them.

Simply buy and hold While mining is the safest and, in some ways, simplest way to earn Bitcoin, it involves too much work and is out of reach for the majority of us due to the cost of electricity and specialized computer hardware. Make it simple for yourself, just enter the amount you want from your bank, click "buy," then sit back and observe as your investment increases in line with the price change to prevent all of this. This is known as exchanging and occurs on several exchange platforms that are currently available, with the capacity to trade between numerous different fiat currencies (USD, AUD, GBP, etc.) and various cryptocurrency coins (Bitcoin, Etherium, Litcoin, etc.).

Trade Bitcoin

If you are familiar with stocks, bonds, or forex exchanges, you will have no trouble understanding cryptocurrency trading. There are Bitcoin brokers such as e-social trading and FXTM Markets.There are various options available, including COM. The platforms provide you Bitcoin-fiat or fiat-Bitcoin currency pairs, for instance, BTC-USD, which means exchanging Bitcoins for U.S. Dollars. Keep an eye on price changes to identify the ideal deal according to price fluctuations; the platforms offer pricing among other indicators to provide you with proper trading advice.

Bitcoin as shares

There are other organizations set up to allow you to purchase shares in businesses that invest in bitcoin; these businesses handle the back-and-forth trading while you simply invest and wait for your monthly benefits. These businesses merely pool digital funds from many investors and invest on their behalf.

Why should you buy Bitcoin?

As you can see, investing in Bitcoin necessitates having at least a rudimentary understanding of the currency, as previously explained. It involves risk, just like with all investments! The decision to invest or not depends entirely on the individual. However, if I had to offer advice, I would advocate investing in Bitcoin since, despite the fact that there has only been one significant boom and bust period, it is quite likely that cryptocurrencies will continue to expand. Over the next ten years, will continue to increase in value as a whole. Bitcoin is now the biggest and best-known cryptocurrency, making it a good place to start and the safest bet. Although uncertain in the short term, I anticipate that you will discover cryptocurrency trading to be more profitable than most other endeavors.

Do you want to experiment with Bitcoin? To get started with the Coinbase exchange and receive $10 worth of free Bitcoin, click this link: [http://getstartedwithcoinbase.trade]

About me: I'm only starting out with cryptocurrency and I'm still learning.

Although everything seems to be a fad, a bubble, and overhyped, there is undoubtedly something worth learning more about. I hope this article was helpful and encourage you to check it out for yourself because the best way to learn is to DO it, and a free $10 doesn't hurt. I wish you luck!

Things to Be Aware Of With Bitcoin

Almost everyone is now aware of bitcoins and bitcoin trading. While the majority of people have succeeded with the currency, there are others who have encountered difficulties. Here are some things you should watch out for if you're planning to enter the market:

A bitcoin wallet

The coins must be used using a digital wallet. It could be an app, hardware, or cloud-based. Some Bitcoin businesses assist newcomers by automatically creating their wallets for them. The purses can be kept offline or online. Keep yours online and make sure the password is secure for security reasons. Avoid online wallets since they can be readily compromised. Keep only a certain amount of money within the unit if you must use it.

Where you purchase currency

If you don't want to go the difficult route of mining the coins yourself, you can always purchase them at the market. When making the transaction, be wary of anyone promising to provide you a commission. Be cautious of the website you are purchasing from as well. When dealing with money, stay away from purchasing from unsecure websites. This urges you to only purchase from websites that begin with HTTP instead than HTTPS. By doing this, you may ensure that the web traffic is secured and secure.

Technical information

You don't need to familiarize yourself with the technical details unless you are involved in the currency mining process. If your primary goal is to purchase the coins, you don't need to spend a lot of time worrying about the mining procedure, block size, and other perplexing aspects of the process. To purchase the currency, locate a trustworthy company and submit your order.

Currency fluctuates

Like other currency markets, the Bitcoin market thrives on changes in the price of the coins. You should be aware that the market is comparable to the long-term share buying and selling market. Due to this, unless you want to sell your coins that same day, you shouldn't be overly concerned with price swings. Because Bitcoin value has been increasing annually, you shouldn't panic if you notice a significant price change in a single day.

Despite the fact that this is the case, you need nonetheless be aware of market prices. Regularly browse forums and related locations to determine the current prices of the currencies. Who knows that you might find it profitable to sell it at the current prices?

Reasons Bitcoin Prices Are So Variable

Price variances in the Bitcoin spot price on the Bitcoin trading exchanges is driven by many reasons. Volatility is assessed in classic markets by the Volatility Index, also called the CBOE Volatility Index (VIX). Since cryptocurrency is still in its early stages as a real asset class, volatility in Bitcoin does not yet present a fully accepted index. However, we do understand that Bitcoin is capable of volatility in the form of 10x price adjustments relative to the US dollar over a relatively short period of time. In this article are just a handful of the various factors in back of Bitcoin's volatility:

1. Negative prices have an effect on the rate of ownership.

News situations that frighten Bitcoin users consist of geopolitical incidents and statements by government authorities that Bitcoin is most likely to be controlled. Bitcoin's first adopters covered many mal actors, generating headline news stories that created worst fears in investors. Headline-producing Bitcoin news includes the bankruptcy of Mt. Gox in early 2014 and that of the South Korean market exchange Yapian Youbit, as well as other stories like the high-profile use of Bitcoin in drug transactions via Silk Road that came to an end when the FBI shut down the market in October 2013. All these occurrences and the general public panic that ensued forced the value of Bitcoins compared to fiat currencies down quickly. Nevertheless, Bitcoin polite investors viewed all those events as proof that the marketplace was growing, generating the value of Bitcoins vs the US dollar substantially back up in the brief period instantly following the information events.

2. Bitcoin's recognized worth changes.

One cause why Bitcoin might change against fiat stock markets is the recognized store of value vs the fiat money. Bitcoin has elements that make it comparable to gold. It is ruled by a design resolution by the developers of the core technology to max capacity its creation to a fixed amount, 21 million BTC. Because this differs significantly from the exchange of fiat currency, which is managed by government agencies that seek to preserve low inflation, high employment, and reasonable growth through investment in capital assets, traders may allocate more or less of their assets directly to Bitcoin as economies developed with fiat currency show signs of strength or weakness.

3. Too much deviation from awareness of the value and market-making technology of Bitcoin.

Different perceptions of the implicit value of the cryptocurrency as a store of value and value converter have a significant role in the volatility of the bitcoin market. A store of value is the action by which an asset can easily be profitable in the future thanks to certain predictability. A valuable item can be kept and changed for something better or more useful in the future. A value transfer technique is any method or procedure used to transfer assets of the type of estates from one entity to another. Although Bitcoin is now an unclear store of value due to its impredicability, it ensures almost frictionless value transfer. As these two factors differ from the US dollar and other fiat foreign currencies, we can see that Bitcoin's value can change based on current events very much like we observe with fiat stock markets.

4. Small-scale value to embrace currency owners.

The degree to which Bitcoin volatility is driven by holders of extremely large percentages of the currency's entire tradable flow is also debatable. It is not immediately clear how Bitcoin traders with recent holdings of more than $10 million would eliminate a position that was equivalent to a fiat position without significantly altering the market. Since Bitcoin's quantity is comparable to a small cap stock, it has not yet reached the market ownership prices necessary to provide option value to large Bitcoin owners.

Purchase a Bitcoin

Without a question, bitcoin trading is gradually taking the world of trade by storm. There is some hype that claims bitcoin trading can be risky and difficult, but in reality, obtaining bitcoins is much simpler than you might expect.

Here are some simple steps for purchasing bitcoin:

- Locate a wallet

First and foremost, you need to locate an e-wallet. It is essentially a retailer or software provider where bitcoins can be purchased, stored, and traded. You may effortlessly use it on your desktop, laptop, and even mobile devices.

Please Register

The next step is to register with E-Wallet. You will create an account that will enable you to store your bitcoins. You will have the option to convert your local currency into bitcoin through the electronic wallet trader. Therefore, you can buy more bitcoins if you have more local currency.

Connect Your Banking Account

The trader must link his bank account with his trading account after signing up. For this reason, several verification steps must be carried out. Once the verifications have been completed, you may begin buying bitcoins and get things going.

Purchasing and Selling

Your bank account will be debited once you have completed your first purchase, and you will then receive your bitcoins. Selling is carried out in the same manner as buying. Remember that the price of bitcoin changes frequently. Your electronic wallet will display the current exchange rate for you. You should be aware of the rate before making a purchase.

The Bitcoin mining process

There is still another method by which you can buy bitcoins. The process is referred to as mining. Bitcoin mining is similar to finding gold in a mine. However, just as mining gold requires a lot of time and effort, the same is true for mining bitcoins. To win free bitcoins, you must correctly complete a sequence of mathematical calculations created by computer algorithms. This is practically hard for a beginner. Traders must open a number of order books in order to finish the mathematical calculations. You don't need to invest any money in this process to win bitcoins because it is only a network that allows free bitcoin wins. The miners must run software in order to earn bitcoins through mining.

A digital money that will be around for a very long time is bitcoin. The trading of bitcoin has increased ever since it was introduced and is still popular today. In addition, as Bitcoin has grown in popularity, its value has increased. It is a new kind of currency that many traders find appealing simply because of its earning potential. In some locations, using bitcoin to buy goods is even practiced. Numerous online retailers now accept bitcoin for in-person purchases as well. There will be a lot of demand for bitcoin in the future, so purchasing them won't be a bad idea.

www.ingramcontent.com/pod-product-compliance
Lightning Source LLC
Chambersburg PA
CBHW050358120526
44590CB00015B/1737